Black Birds : Blue Horse

Natalie Peeterse

AN ELEGY

Black Birds : Blue Horse

Natalie Peeterse

AN ELEGY

WINNER OF THE 2011 GOLD LINE PRESS CHAPBOOK COMPETITION

IN POETRY

GOLD LINE PRESS
LOS ANGELES

In memory of Nicole Dial, who was killed in the Logar Province of Afghanistan on August 13, 2008 while working for the International Rescue Committee.

Copyright © 2012 by Natalie Peeterse

All rights reserved

Printed by Lulu in the United States of America

Book Design & Artwork by Richelle Gribble
Gold Line Press logo by Nicholas Katzban

Gold Line Press publishes chapbooks of poetry and fiction with the aim to promote the work of emerging writers as well as showcase the chapbook form. The goal of our annual competition is to support exceptional writers through the publication and broad distribution of their work. Gold Line Press is associated with the University of Southern California's Ph.D. program in Literature and Creative Writing.

ISBN-13: 978-1-105-54360-9

Gold Line Press
3501 Trousdale Parkway, THH 431
Los Angeles, CA 90089-0354

www.goldlinepress.com

GOLD LINE PRESS
LOS ANGELES

because even the tiny banquet of a spider

is enough to upset the entire equilibrium of the sky

> -Federico Garcia Lorca

To whom do we tell what happened on the earth, for whom do we place everywhere huge mirrors in the hope that they will be filled up and will stay so?

> -Czeslaw Milosz

One two : three four :   then two more :

gunshots.   I wake to some kind of tactical

counter-terrorism exercise, or some kind

of national emergency   or

the dead body of a girl on the glittering road.

Either way, wind outside.   In waves.

The heat blasts on   and

off. I roll over and answer the phone : *hello?*

It is the voice of my father saying

that you're gone or that we've lost you or something—

that burns.   That is a burning *no*.

When I see *your* father next, he'll be holding a book

you made as a girl. A yellow duck hand-drawn on the cover.

He will hold it all that day.

The only thing I know how to do is leave

: to wander—but even as I begin I am refused.

The cab driver throws me out after a block—

he refuses to ferry me across this city with one voice,

consoles someone softly on his cell in Arabic with another.

I walk to catch the last green line train

but miss it—there are crickets with dark armored shells

      everywhere. You might have called tonight

a landscape of pissing multitudes with one voice,

the heart of a feasting spider with another.

Voices come in all directions after a certain

hour and the oily clap of bus breaks, helicopter blades

become a slide of time :   the softest snow.

Did you hear again a man lit himself

on fire in front of the White House ?   Watch

as the fire spiders from his clothes

to his skin. It is so clever : fire—

so candid and without regret. So like our pink

likenesses : a lobster-elephant-Pepto-Bismol-duck-billed

reflection back at me where nothing fits, bodies

do not settle and if you notice

they do not have   hands the way we do

when we speak of them.

Tonight the moon came up anyway—

blurred over a row of abandoned boxcars and a wobbly wire fence.

Its glitter is almost indistinguishable from the new streetlights

and glowing marquees over on H St. that it rises against.

You are not here. Only past.

There is only before now : only slips and

shapes : the stars look as if they have been put into jars

      and shaken—

they hang like bullied children.

The tourists like junebugs, we always said : easy enough to capture

and kill. They'd go for pairs

: hold one down   and pester the other.

The crackle as they pull two wings from the amber body.

Kick and wiggle, kick and wiggle

go the instruments of our inner lives.

In this wilderness they await—

golden eyed and hungry for the real soldiers.

The ones who will embrace us : who wave back

from outside the crumbling city.

Who know what children know : that the world spins

on and on   on its copper axis. That the wind

is a blue horse come to carry us

on from the world as it is: sunsoaked

and snaking : cruel—

        not at its end :

In the darkness a message from the yellowgray sea

: planes snake through the fog first revealing

a wing. Then the red/black stripe

of industry and then they fall

one by   one nose first : hundreds

we slide the tarmac—

if the true life is waiting for us in the next world

      with you

then the silver tip of a banking wing is just scattered

wreckage the swell of collision : a spill—

In the excavation each line will mean something—

a dim arch, a cutting edge, a yellow core.

The stark face and dark eyes of a bird

will look up at rows of gritting teeth and your

shoulderblade : your emptied days

compacted like sand. Into sand. Of sand :

the architecture of the plain

of your beginning   and your ending

hinges on the beak of a stellar's jay

and the barrel of a dusty Kalashnikov—

    but all I can see now is the open curl

of your palm : the light of the cerulean world reflected there.

I flip a buffalo nickel through my fingers

        just to watch it.

Just to watch it, not to think about the mess.

I'm on the 14th St. bus with the feel of everyone's

hands on the poles and in the seats.

The mothers hassle the children into place.

The old lady in rags : an open wound drips

from her shoulder. And me

with our secret together—

The lighted tips of the National Cathedral kick in the sky.

Dark trees lean in. I walk west on Kenyon.

A young man steps around the corner at 18th St.

with purpose. He approaches and then the cold feel

of gun to my skin under a blinking streetlight.

He is young　　　　　but not afraid—

his eyes are too similar to the others

in the world news photos　　　: remorseless and

tired they peer into the camera.

Here is my money, I say, and hand him your sandstorm.

Twenty.   Or twenty-five.

The bullets went straight through   your body.

It must have been so loud.

I've decided   you didn't feel a thing

on that road south of Kabul, on your way

back to the city to continue the work.

Of saving?

Not even the shards of hot glass from the windshield

through which the bullets passed

as they burned into your face.

At the equinox of a stranger and the self

day and night are everywhere of equal length, it seems—

and so things are possible

and so   precarious the ghetto doors

blown open in the running wind.

Plywood thumps and booms all day here

and all these baby girls—

their voices like swallows. The tiny hinges

of a thousand shoes and precious ankles

move forward :   to the windows of our fear.

Press your face to the glass like a girl does

when she can't sleep : the clap of so many wings.

I wonder that one of them will find you out there,

keeping in its beak a small sound like a small

fire in a box　　　　by the night.

That its limbs will bend like beams

to be close enough to the rim of things.

To travel with you.

Each night that passes is just one

in the invisible flocks of blackbirds that swirl

out　　　　into the zoos of the discarded—

a sweet wilderness of strobe lights and blue smoke

that curls into the empty tin of a city marching on.

Tonight, though, the streets are shiny and unencumbered by your eyes—

slicked over with doubt : that cruel biology of the spirit.

And the waiting for you, and then

things to cut the pain   of waiting.

I step onto the escalator as it scrolls down into the subway

and creaks like a tree in the wind.

Terracotta-colored, honeycomb-shaped tiles are everywhere

in this city : a pattern one cannot help but repeat—

      foot to tile, foot to tile.

Watch all the waiting passengers sway

against the lighted windows of each subway car.

They must understand that at any time   it can come—

lucky then that one can pass easily as a ghost here—

to wander perfectly unseen as the world bangs

and brims in the wind : a quick alien

always on the sharp edge of sleep.

They come and go   ceaselessly.

They rise like the thin slivers of sprouts

from underground. They hold babies wrapped

like presents : eyes to the ground. To the rumble.

All the while the neighborhood dogs run and

bawl, and the world is ticking   ticks.

Just as anywhere : we all crawl

home in swirls of dust and the clouds above

the clouds are at the hem of your skirt.

They inch closer like the sun on someone else's barren

landscape. Like the magnified shadows on the back of all the gray houses

just now, saying :   *wait.*

That the perfect city glitters : each of us breathing

slow, tranquil inhalations to start the sun

moving   because what we see coming

is probably nothing   : the weather of seahorses

all the truest birds closing in   so darkly—

That we must push through this place, our names

brambled, if spoken : the horizon pinched into a slim bit of a thing.

And hope that they will always come for us—

the little blue mirrors of mercy, the stillness

between you   and the blade.

I see him out of the corner of my eye.

A horse stretches his legs out over the arid land—

      an azure horse with a gray mane.

Even blurred like this you can see he is too thin—

coarse hair and common water : the cloud

of a document that empties into a pool of plain,

cold water.   The weight on a shoe.

We bend in under his weather.

The heavy blanket of your absence now

folded perfectly in one hand, and the other filled

with worldly things : hooves and nickels, their brittle noises.

No one is listening, you say.

    No one is watching—

and both of your hands open again to reveal

a million ochre-bellied ants with the tiniest black legs

shuffling : they move and work endlessly.

Your armies form a river around your wrists—

In each ant glows the belly of a gas stove burning
in these homes, in place of any other kind of heat.
The oven door open and the babies asleep nearby.
Each ant a backdraft, and all of them together
the ashes of our identities carried out with us
        into the night. Some—
move languidly   in orange loops,
some scamper forward faster than footsteps.

Is this the demarcation between each of us—

the buzz and bend of a stranger's voice as it passes by your ear?

As one says—

    I see you there.

You are so big against the sidewalk

as the men lean against wrought iron gates—

they smoke and chatter as if things will never unfold

onto these streets though they are always on the edge

    of flight : quick as the blue wind : galloping.

The city has taken it back.

I get to the apartment and inside a scattering

        of someone else's things—

busted suitcases, florescent stickers lighting the wall.

The sound of the door unhinged   behind me.

By the bed a pair of tiny white shoes

and another pair in watermelon green

and pink. Abandoned on the bed : a blue plastic pony

with a glittering mane of fake silk.

On the stove an old cast iron skillet, the lid mismatched.

Something forgotten inside.

That your voice was sometimes a horrible labor—

you railed against anyone who might

still :   the truth is : the sky holds over its kin

and its forgotten no matter how far we wander.

No matter the names of things : Afghanistan

: District of Columbia : Pul-i-Alam : home.

In the morning a jar of sand on my doorstep—

an entire population of little nameless particles

crushed in together, especially where the glass bells.

I want to take it down to Pennsylvania Avenue

and shake it into the street for blocks and blocks—

        unhurried : to watch each bit

of intermittent light. To watch the road to Kabul

open up before me—

Acknowledgments

"Tonight the streets shiny and unencumbered by your eyes"; "All the waiting passengers sway"; "The heavy blanket of your constant absence now"; and "In each ant glows the belly of a gas stove burning" appeared in Strange Machine, Winter 2009 issue.

Thank you to the Caldera Arts Center in Sisters, Oregon for the valuable residency.

Thank you to my readers and friends, Ken White, Rob Schlegel, Chris Dombrowski, Megan Gannon, Miles Waggener, Claire Hibbs Cheff, M.L. Smoker, and most especially, Amy Ratto Parks.

Natalie Peeterse has an MFA from the University of Montana. Her poetry has appeared in *Blackbird, Sonora Review* and *Strange Machine*, among other journals. Her poems have appeared in *I Go to the Ruined Place: Contemporary Poems in Defense of Global Human Rights* (Lost Horse Press) and other anthologies. She has been a fellow with the Arizona Commission on the Arts, a participant at the Squaw Valley Community of Writers, and was most recently an artist in residence at the Caldera Institute in central Oregon. She lives in Missoula, MT with her family.

Photo Credit: Adam Sings in the Timber